ASKA'S ANIMALS

Paintings by Warabé Aska   Poetry by David Day

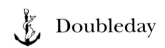 Doubleday

A Doubleday Book for Young Readers

Published in Canada by
Doubleday Canada Limited
105 Bond Street
Toronto, Ontario M5B 1Y3

Published in the United States by
Delacorte Press
Bantam Doubleday Dell Publishing Group, Inc.
666 Fifth Avenue
New York, New York 10103

Doubleday and the portrayal of an anchor with a dolphin
are trademarks of Bantam Doubleday Dell Publishing Group, Inc.

Canadian Cataloguing in Publication Data

Aska, Warabé
    Aska's animals

ISBN 0-385-25315-X

1. Aska, Warabé.   2. Animals in art.   I. Day, David, 1947-   . II. Title.

ND249.A84A4 1991   759.11   C91-093679-X

Library of Congress Cataloging (U.S.A.) in Publication Data applied for

Design by Ross Mah Design Associates
Printed and bound in Hong Kong

November 1991
10987654321

Where did the animals come from?
What god or spirit shaped them?

It's a guessing game for you and me,
Imagining how the beasts began.

The first horses were made of sea foam.

They rode their waves to the beaches
Then broke loose and dashed for the shore.

Wild horses, raging with pride—
Look how much of the untamed sea

Is within them still.

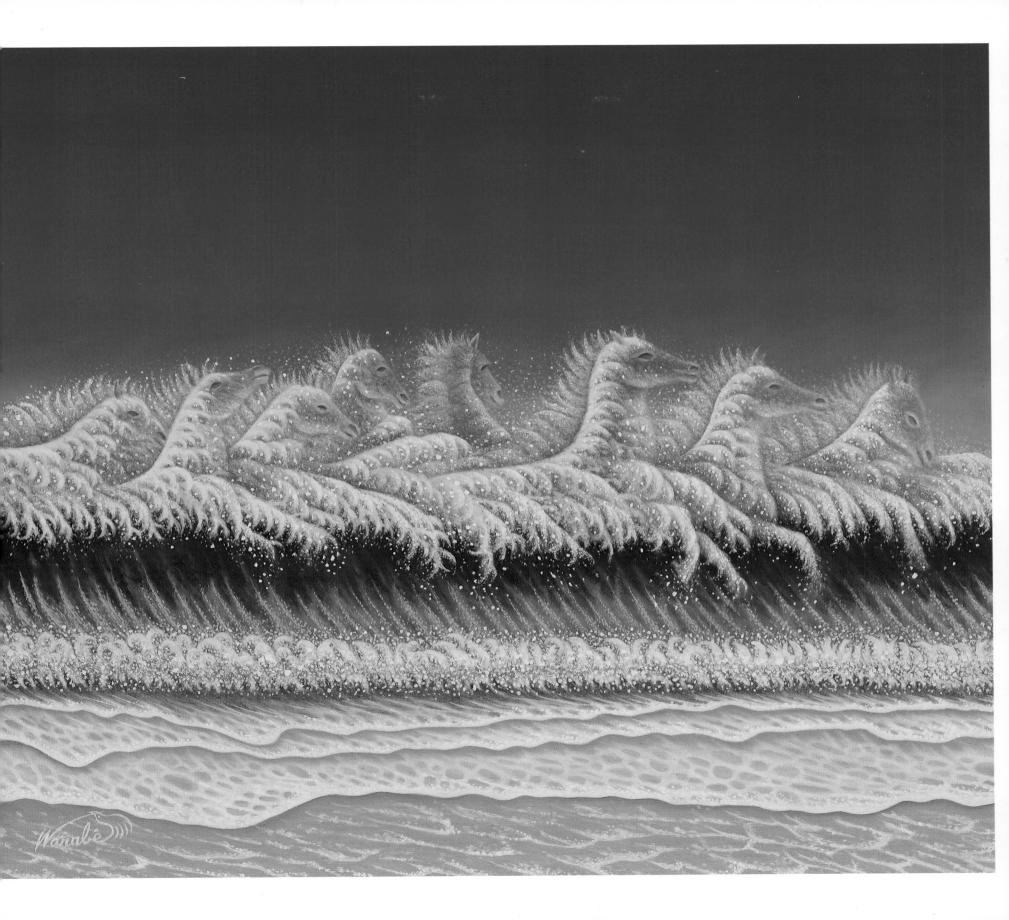

Branching antlers are a clue
To the mysteries of the deer.

Gentle, fleet-footed, leaping with delight,

They were once tree spirits
That were restless for flight.

6

"In dreamtime," the kangaroo explained,
"We were made of gum tree sap and red clay.
   Then, we were hidden away in caverns far below."

"So, we leapt and thumped and shook the earth
   Until the rock ceiling cracked.
   And out we sprang, like a river in full flow."

8

Racing over grass like frantic ghosts,
Hares go mad in the moonlight.

For the moon was once the skylight door
Through which the first hares toppled.

Each night they chase it, hoping to return home.

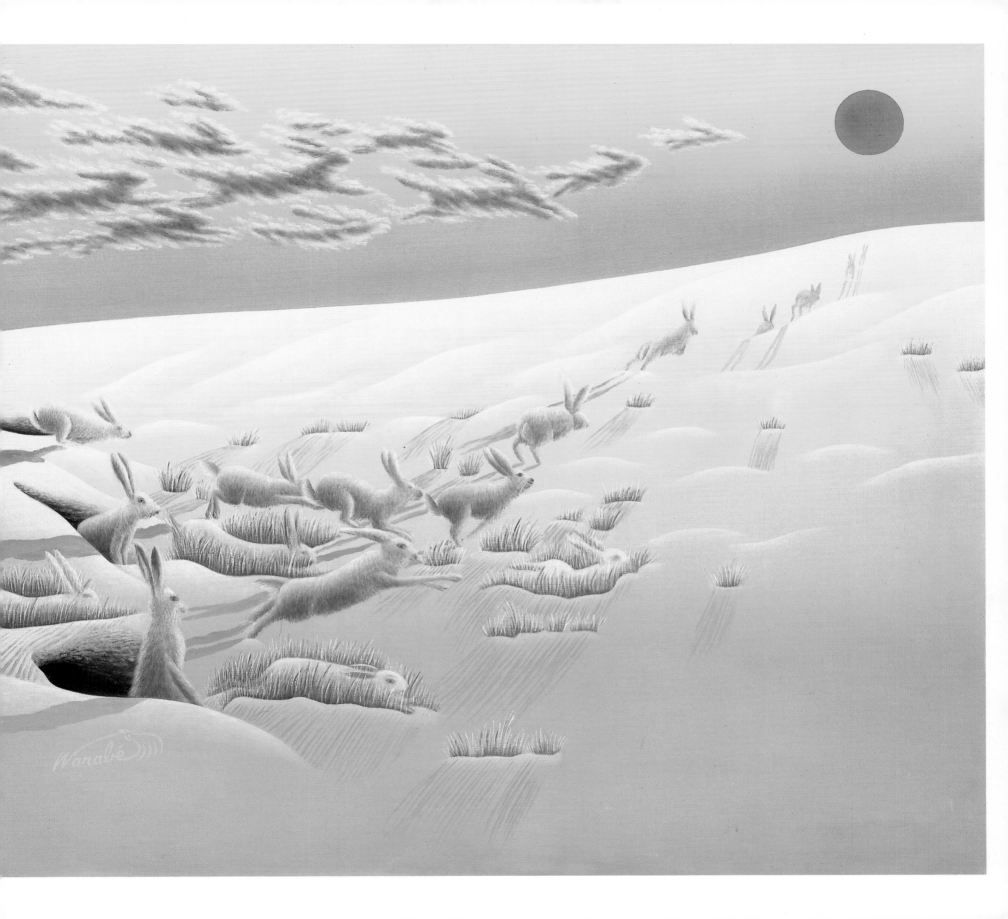

Sand-coloured and humped like the dunes,
Camels rest beneath a pale moon.

The first camels were shaped by the lonely song
Of the wind whispering over shifting sands.

Hunters of the hot grasslands
The golden lions make their stand—

Shaggy-maned and fierce as that first pride
Forged long ago in the glowing furnace of the sun.

There can be no doubt about hippopotamuses,
Those happy, lazy, yawning monsters.

Shaped out of great lumps of muck by childish gods,
Then left to bake in the sun,

Hippos are monuments to the glories of mud.

The sun looked down on paradise.
One glance turned the forest pool to liquid gold.

Then, a gentle breeze stirred the pool to life,
And the first tigers rippled into the world.

Elephants in joyful celebration
Trumpet loudly in praise of light.

Watch in wonder as the gates of heaven open.

At the moment of creation, could they have been
Anything less than trumpeting angels

With wide wings instead of those huge ears?

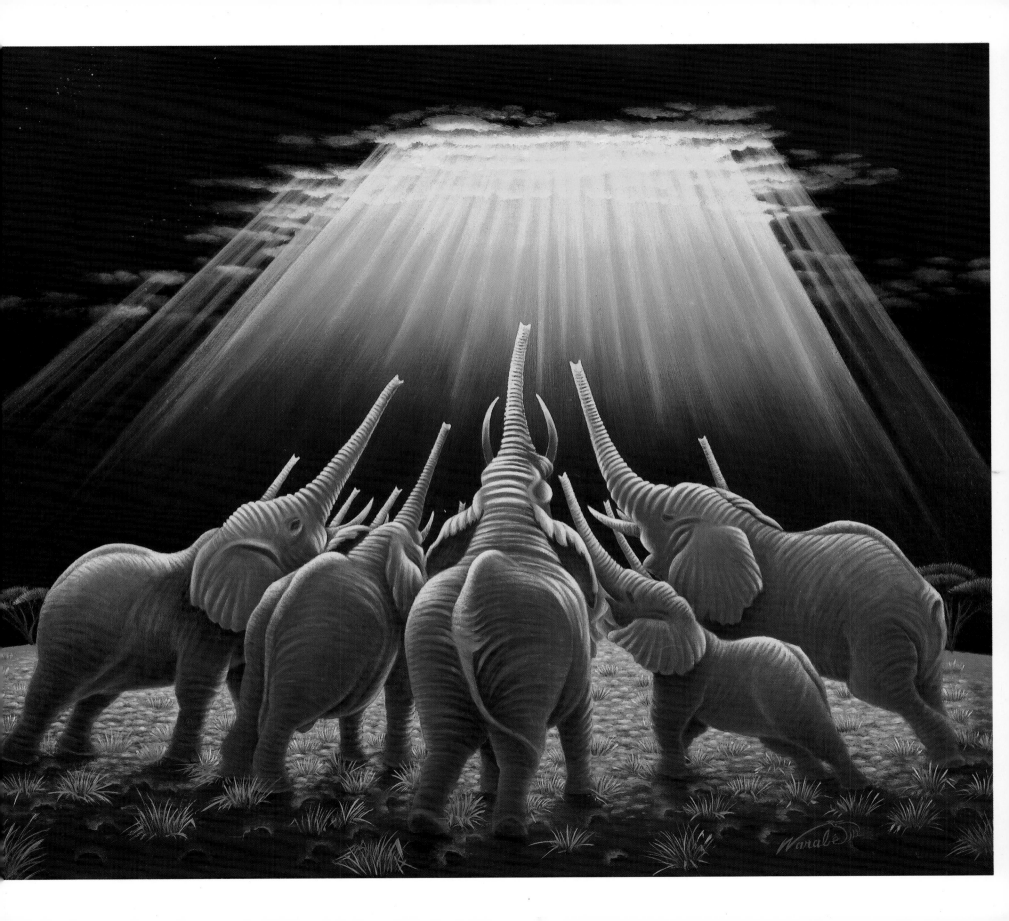

The trouble with contemplating giraffes
Is that watching them can wear you down.

Who made them so high?

The truth is, giraffes were invented by forest pygmies
To stop the tall trees stealing all their sunlight.

The story of the musk ox is simply absurd:
One day, a herd of haystacks suddenly sprouted legs,
Then, standing up, marched north in search of snow.

After the age of volcanoes, the lava flows
Cooled their stony fingers in the sea.

Time and lapping water shaped these rocks.
While the god of crocodiles watched, and gave them life.

One look at the crocodile's smile tells
What all his victims know:

The crocodile's heart is still made of stone.

When zebras come to drink at dusk,
Watch the rippling dance of shadow and light.

It's easy enough to understand
How this water music came galloping to life.

The first polar bears were as light as snowflakes.

In bright flurries, they fell glittering from the sky
Onto mountain tops, where they gathered and grew.

Then, huge and unstoppable as an avalanche,
They roared down the mountains, and toppled into the sea.

The world is wide and full of wonders.
Imagining beginnings is a never-ending game.

These are just a few magical beasts.
How many more can you name?